Deep Lane

ALSO BY MARK DOTY

POETRY

A Swarm, A Flock, A Host (with Darren Waterston)
Paragon Park
Fire to Fire: New and Selected Poems
School of the Arts
Source
Sweet Machine
Atlantis
My Alexandria
Bethlehem in Broad Daylight
Turtle, Swan

PROSE

What Is the Grass (forthcoming)
The Art of Description
Dog Years
Still Life with Oysters and Lemon
Firebird: A Memoir
Heaven's Coast

Deep Lane

POEMS

Mark Doty

W. W. NORTON & COMPANY

NEW YORK • LONDON

For information about permission to reproduce selections from this
book, write to Permissions, W. W. Norton & Company, Inc.,
500 Fifth Avenue, New York, NY 10110

For information about special discounts for bulk purchases, please
contact W. W. Norton Special Sales at specialsales@wwnorton.com or
800-233-4830

Manufacturing by Courier Westford
Book design by Brooke Koven
Production manager: Anna Oler

Library of Congress Cataloging-in-Publication Data

Doty, Mark.
[Poems. Selections]
Deep lane : poems / Mark Doty.—First edition.
     pages ; cm
ISBN 978-0-393-07023-1 (hardcover)
I. Title.
PS3554.O798A6 2015
811'.54—dc23
                                        2015000660

W. W. Norton & Company, Inc.
500 Fifth Avenue, New York, N.Y. 10110
www.wwnorton.com

W. W. Norton & Company Ltd.
Castle House, 75/76 Wells Street, London W1T 3QT

1 2 3 4 5 6 7 8 9 0

FOR ALEXANDER

CONTENTS

ACKNOWLEDGMENTS

SOME OF THESE poems appeared previously in the following magazines:

Four Two Nine: Ars Poetica: 14th Street Gym, To Jackson Pollock, Not Without (as "To the Eye")

American Poetry Review: Crystal, Deep Lane (*When I'm down on my knees . . .*), Little Mammoth, Underworld, What Is the Grass?, Deep Lane (*Trying to pick . . .*)

The Financial Times: Immanence

Granta: Apparition (*I'm carrying . . .*)

Hunger Mountain: Deep Lane (*June 23rd . . .*)

New England Review: The King of Fire Island

New Republic: Perfect Repose

New South: Ineradicable Music

The New Yorker: Deep Lane (*November and this road's . . .*), Pescadero

The New York Times: The Lesson

Ploughshares: Deep Lane (*I'm resting on a bench . . .*)

Plume: God-Box

Poem-a-Day, published by the Academy of American
   Poets: Robert Harms Paints the Surface of Little
   Fresh Pond, Spent, This Your Home Now, Verge

Sleet: Robinson Jeffers

The Southampton Review: Deep Lane (*Into Eden . . .*)

Tricycle: Amagansett Cherry

"Deep Lane (*I'm resting on a bench . . .*)" appeared in
   The Best American Poetry 2014.

Deep Lane

As the traveler who has lost his way
throws his reins on his horse's neck, and
trusts to the instinct of the animal to find
his road, so must we do with the divine
animal who carries us through this world.
—Ralph Waldo Emerson

All right then, I'll go to Hell.
—Mark Twain

DEEP LANE

When I'm down on my knees pulling up wild mustard
by the roots before it sets seed, hauling the old ferns
further into the shade, I'm talking to the anvil of darkness:

break-table, slab no blow could dent
rung with the making, and out of that chop and rot
comes the fresh surf of the lupines.

When the shovel slips into white root-flesh,
into the meat coursing with cool water,
when I'm grubbing on my knees, what is the hammer?

Dusky skin of the tuber, naked worms
who write on the soil every letter,
my companion blind, all day we go digging,

harrowing, rooting deep. Spade-plunge
and trowel, sweet turned-down gas flame
slow-charring carbon, out of which sprouts

the wild unsayable.
Beauty's the least of it:
you get ready,

like Deborah, who used to garden in the dark,
hauling out candles and a tall glass of what she said
    was tea,
and digging and reading and studying in the dirt.

She'd bring a dictionary. If study is prayer, she said, I'm
    praying.
If you've already gone down to the anvil, if you've rested
    your face
on that adamant, maybe you're already changed.

DEEP LANE

June 23rd, evening of the first fireflies,
we're walking in the cemetery down the road,
and I look up from my distracted study of whatever,

an unfocused gaze somewhere a few feet in front of my
    shoes,

and see that Ned has run on ahead
with the champagne plume of his tail held especially high,
his head erect,

which is often a sign that he has something he believes he is
    not allowed to have,

and in the gathering twilight (what is it that is gathered,
who is doing the harvesting?) I can make out that the long
    horizontal
between his lovely jaws is one of the four stakes planted on
    the slope

to indicate where the backhoe will dig a new grave.

Of course my impulse is to run after him, to replace the
    marker,

out of respect for the rule that we won't desecrate the
    tombs,
or at least for those who knew the woman

whose name inks a placard in the rectangle claimed by the
    four poles

of vanishing—three poles now—and how it's within their
    recollection,
their gathering, she'll live. Evening of memory. Spark-
    lamps in the grass.
I stand and watch him go in his wild figure eights,

I say, You run, darling, you tear up that hill.

DEEP LANE

We began to think the white fish individual
—the one of the pair who'd struggled, after all,
when our pond's colder water shocked

and he lay pulsing in the shallows
till we thought him all but gone . . .
Then simply drew himself up,

if that were something a fish
could do, and swam away.
A heron ate his mate.

He surfaced in March,
after his first season
entombed in the bottom-mud,

unscathed, a four-inch emperor
in his white silk coat,
insignia of the kingdom

splashed over his back
the color of candied orange rind.
He'd nose up out of the lily-murk

when our shadows crossed his borders,
push to the edge to open the translucent
white ring of his mouth over and over

as if begging . . . As if! Seems to want,
seems to feel. But as we knew him
semblance fell away: We felt the presence

of the soul of him, if soul could be
understood as specificity,
so that when he himself was swallowed

—white appetite perched on the roof,
bill raised to the air, the throat unrelenting—

the absence in the pond grew resonant,
a sort of empty ringing. Where were the details then,
the gestures that had marked him?

Heaped stones and elder, mullein and pokeweed . . .
How can I take any pleasure in this garden?

DEEP LANE

Into Eden came the ticks,
princes of this world,
heat-seeking, tiny, multitudinous

—Lord, why have you given them
a heart, a nervous system, a lit microchip
of a—brain, is it?—if not to invite Manicheanism;

hard to believe the force that shaped the mild tortoise
traversing the undergrowth with smallest steps,
the sway-necked lily,

hard to countenance that same mind
dotting paradise with pinhead demons
wanting nothing but to gorge, to suck

beyond the dreams of their hell-brothers
the mosquitoes—implacable, without boundary,
pure appetite. I wouldn't know anything about that.

DEEP LANE

Down there the little star-nosed engine of desire
at work all night, secretive: in the morning

a new line running across the wet grass, near the surface,

like a vein. Don't you wish the road of excess
led to the palace of wisdom, wouldn't that be nice?

It leads to this shingled cottage,
blue-shuttered, where the lilacs rustle and swell in the
    warm dark,

and what are those birds
who won't be still after midnight? Furtive lamp burning in
    each window,

long after the good solid neighbors are asleep,

and while they're dreaming I'm up all night
in my tunnel of lack, keeping company,

in love with smoke-swirl in a glass ball,
worrying at the entrances to the underworld . . .

Until I stumble out, at dawn,
after the rainy night when the wind's blown open the gate,

a night alone but in no sense solitary, since it was given
    over
to incompletion, all the objects of desire

dulled now and drained. Wanting nothing, Sir,
was that what you always had in mind for me?

CRYSTAL

He rubbed the clear envelope with the backside of a spoon
—milk-sheen feldspar brought up from the dark,
flawed angular interior of the quartz I loved as a child,

light-catching fractures revealed as it's turned—
and lifted sharp little stars into the hollow
of the syringe with an angle-cut straw,

and sucked through the needle an equal volume
of heated water, shook the filled instrument
till the crystals dissolved, holding it a while over the warm
    bulb

of a lamp, and tied my arm with a piece of stretchy plastic,
maybe a leather belt or a necktie, I don't remember.
He said, *You'll probably cough, that's normal.*

Then began the finding of the vein, no reason
in the world you'd understand the eros of this
unless you'd also . . . Then he entered me, so to speak,

though I knew I was the one walking
without hesitation through the door he held open,
and *in a moment* I want to write I did cough

but that is suddenly the crux of it:
moment, what is that? Time peeled back
its own clear skin, a jellyfish

inverting itself
in a convulsive act of self-propulsion.
What did I feel? Absolute rightness coursing

without concurrent pain regret the sense of dread
—do I mean the sense of *dead*,
the already worn out,

choices made, ends accomplished?
He filled the syringe
with the shattered stuff of possibility,

I went riding all night on Tear Me Apart Road,
midnight all night, slick gates smashed by storm cloud,
the hour one roaring bell, and I could live inside

that never-ceasing, further, long after
I thought there was anything more to let go, I
let go the reins and the wheel,

the stays and the cautions,
consequentiality. Put your boot to what's left
of my softness, Sir: an anemone

swallowing its own blossom, and what lies
on the other side of that? The what-I-lack-speech-for,
an astonishingly present tense

blown open seven ways from the hour,
I am refined, my base elements
burnt away, or am I now nothing more

than base: purified in the smith's fire
till I'm heat and light and no weight,
a coursing fluid thing without encumbrance,

I can't stop speaking, though I'm saying nothing:
the words want to come flying, habit and vestige.
No time now for speech, and isn't this

what my whole life's wanted, to go flying
past the words that have been my signature
and trade? So that I might arrive on the far bank

of what could be said, and how impossibly lovely
the unsustainable, the who knew, the ferocity
of the animal in whose furred and rutting presence

you became real to me, second person, strange little king
in your translucent architectonics, your crumbling
salts that remade or did you release me? So I began

to offer up through my body and its ministrations
its worship its lights its weather rising and falling tide
I began to offer service and obeisance I began to rock

—I could never stop my thigh from rocking—
and to speak the beast-speech of my birthright.
I mean to say the surge identified itself to me

as divine, but to whom could this poem pray?
Freed animal, lost head, pure creature, sudden musical
    phrase
not passing in time but hanging, and caught within that

want without fulfillment or satisfaction,
almost without object, refined,
crystalline, become the impossible white.

PERFECT REPOSE

Turning so effortlessly
you wouldn't call it that, what they do,
sliding easily over,

a kind of oscillation,
on their sides, most of them,
floating together

in their troop,
perhaps twenty-five of them
just off the pier, though

you couldn't count them,
the sea lions: they curve around
one another, two break away,

one joins, the group drifts
with the tide. Whose flipper
or tail raised to the sun,

whose head lifted out of the green?
They lie a little beneath
the surface, now and then

turning the face up to breathe,
which is suddenly how you know
they're asleep: simultaneous,

intimate, soft plosive, a little wet,
and though one coughs now and then
—water in the nose?—

the single thing they make of many,
still and always moving,
as if air were also a wave

now arrived at the drifting shore of—
what pronoun? I mean *thou*
all breathe in again at once.

DEEP LANE

I'm resting on a bench in the cemetery
while Ned scrawls his self-delighted wild-boy trace
over the slopes of grass, but we can't stay long,

since it's a day I need to go into the city,
and when I stand up suddenly my left leg's half a foot
lower than my right, because I've stepped into the sunken,

newly filled grave of one Herbert Meyer.
I don't know it then, but that's when the wind
blows up from beneath; I think I'm just off balance,

and make a joke of it later, telling people my day began
with falling into a grave, and where can you go from there?
Later a storm blows down the moraine,

crisp and depth-charged with ozone and exhilaration,
chills my face and arms with a wind I've already met,
winds up the lanes and rattles the cups in the cabinet,

bends the beautyberry and Joe Pye weed down
in the direction of beautiful supplication;
the maple and walnut sway in the highest regions of
    themselves,

leaves circling in air like the great curtain of bubbles
blown by the humpback to encircle the delicious schools . . .
Blows in my sleep and blows while I'm cooking,

blows while I read and when I kiss does it ever
blow then, the wind not particular to Mr. Meyer
nor anyone else, and thus the nervy thrill

of its invitation: to be unbound, not at all
what you thought, to rush up from the sinking earth
on a gust of investigation: now go be

the crooked little house, and the cracks in the shingles,
tunnel your hour as the mouse in the stale loaf, fly back
to the strong hands of the baker, further back into the
    wheat,

forward into the belly of the mouse-child,
what reason to ever end? I know one:
if you don't hold still, you can have joy after joy,

but you can't stay anywhere to love. That's the price,
that rib-rattling wind waiting to sweep you up,

that's the price the wind pays.

THE KING OF FIRE ISLAND

Hard by our fence in tea-dance light,
he seemed the very model of his kind:

a buck in velvet at the garden rim,
bronze lightly shagged, split thumbs

of antlers budding. That odd way deer hold
extra still, as though there were degrees

of stasis. We were objects of his regal,
mild regard.
                    Did I really say *tea*?

Measure the afternoon by a bar event?
Here it's a fixed point, gnomon

of the day; our island's scattered men gather,
near seven, and stand with cocktails

in the thick of buzzing bodies, intent
in quick talk, though their subtle eyes

won't miss a trick. Here, after all,
tea dance *started*—wise strategy

for an island with no streetlamps,
boardwalks pitching along the dunes:

scary, after drinks, far better navigated
before nightfall.
                              He stepped toward us,

an unexpected lurch, and then
we saw: one front leg merely tapered

to a whisper, like the torso
of a cartoon ghost. No hoof.

He gladly accepted a carrot,
a gesture plainly familiar.

Where else could he have lived?
No cars, no hunting, visitors

who'd bring him kitchen scraps,
nothing to trouble but cameras

buzzing their automatic flash,
or dance music booming

from some big box rental.
And ticks; he wore a small crown

of swollen passengers
between his two brave ears,

where he could not bite them,
and no other deer provided

the seemingly secret grooming
they perform. He exhaled a small puff

of carrot-scented wind,
handsome face expressive,

not much in doubt of the human.
We'd see him, evenings, up the walk,

browsing the cranberry bog;
he hauled himself through gardens,

intently working tufts of grass,
muscled shoulder pulling him ahead.

A hoof's a deft accomplishment,
that hard-sheened shoe of blue-black carbon,

but he'd learned to do with what he had.
I brought him celery. He liked

corn silk but not the husks,
and seemed to prefer the leaves

of sassafras, with their faint spice scent;
something—did I imagine it?—

seemed to pass across his gaze
as he took them in, lower jaw working

horizontally, a faint tearing sound,
Then he'd take his tongue to my hands.

They startled me at first, those sucking lips
around my fingertips, careful,

as if he were grooming another
of his kind. I felt I could lay my hand

on that long slope of forehead,
or stroke behind the ears,

though whatever was left
of his wildness needed to stand.

I tried to name him; he wanted no word
from me. More likely I should be subject

to this monarch of holly,
hobbling prince of shadblow grove,

our island's crippled king.
When July mounted to its zenith

his antlers turned in oddly,
each mirroring the other

—wouldn't they collide?
What grows in toward itself,

how can it find company among
its kind? I went looking, spent daylilies

in hand, but if a white tail flashed,
it wasn't his. Paul said, *You can't will him*

to show up. Out there somewhere
in the leaf-realms of August,

lurching alone through all that glory!
In the distance the party thundered,

season climbing to its apogee,

big speakers dragged out to the shore
where midnight lapped the snow fence

and dreamers swayed and danced,
held one another or themselves,

and though the artificial mist tried
to complicate the twittering

skyfield of laser lights,
a real fog put the false to shame.

In November, Paul saw him
grazing a thicket by the yellowing bog.

Not again. Then, late winter,
a hushed, not quite scrutable rumor

on the ferry: a deer's head
floating in the bay, wreathed

with flowers, evidence of—
ritual murder, santería?—

never to be mentioned again.
Bad for business, knowledge

no summer renter required.
My friend? Have I any right

to call him that? He could hardly flee.
But listen:
             I saw my own severed head

slip to the floor, a glazed, paltry thing,
open eye looking up toward—my subjectivity?—

as if through a bloody gel. So much
for the notion you can't die in a dream:

I was the witness I've always been.

Likewise beheaded, would you allow me,
now, to do what I would not

when you were living,
and take in my hands

those twin branches sturdy as oars?
Can't I take hold of you, in the water,

in the dark, floating in the gift
of flowers, not lurching, steady, easy?

Now guide me out of the story, spirit;
I don't know where it is you lead, but I believe.

You must have been weary of that form,
as I grow weary of my head,

and leave it behind—cast-off thing—
and lend my body to your severed crown.

LITTLE MAMMOTH

Mother's milk in my belly

and a little of her shit, too,
so that I might eat

of the sour-green steppes
that opened endlessly

before me, though not long
after I slid into sunlight

and the grass-world I slid
again into the mudhole,

and screamed, and screaming
sucked clay into my trunk

till I lay on the bottom,
my milk-tusks not even

sprouted, a sweet undercoat
of fat ready for my first winter,

and I am still one month old, and
forty thousand years without my mother.

APPARITION

I'm carrying an orange plastic basket of compost
down from the top of the garden—sweet dark,

fibrous rot, promising—when the light changes
as if someone's flipped a switch that does

what? Reverses the day. Leaves chorusing,
dizzy. And then my mother says

—she's been gone more than thirty years,
not her voice, the voice of her in me—

You've got to forgive me. I'm choke and sputter
in the wild daylight, speechless to that:

maybe I'm really crazy now, but I believe
in the backwards morning I am my mother's son,

we are at last equally in love
with intoxication, I am unregenerate,

the trees are on fire, fifty-eight years of lost bells.
I drop my basket and stand struck

in the iron-mouth afternoon. She says
I never meant to harm you. Then

the young dog barks, down by the front gate,
he's probably gotten out, and she says,

calmly, clearly, *Go take care of your baby.*

HUNGRY GHOST

Even if I understood what the teachers said,
that my desire was a thirst
for something beyond forms,

I believed I would be incomplete
if I did not know longing;

I would miss nothing,
wanted to be marked by the passage,
wanted to be inscribed.

And then I was given the key
to a wanting that won't stop as long as I live.

Where was my gracious consent to attachment then?
I was taught to say, Please, Sir,
may I have more? Taught by craving, by the roar

in the blood rising without volition,
no place to stand that did not lean

forward, no still point. I harrowed sleep
and memory, descended into
the purely physical howl of the world,

learned my size in relation to appetite,

from which I could no more step back
than I could change the eyes

through which I read this page.
When I'm gone, will I stop wanting?

Perhaps this is also a form of immortality:
submission to a craving without boundary.

To be ravenous, and lack a mouth.

DEEP LANE

Whose black and yellow signature
unscribbling itself across the path?

The striped snake in the garden loves me
so fiercely she never comes near, she hides

in the stacked flat stones all day, and hopes
a little sun will find her there, just a little.

She's my mother come to look in
on how I'm doing, my secret advocate,

deeply indifferent, entirely benign.
If I dose myself she won't care, she wants me

to be happy, she wants me to take
the course I take. She stands

in a perfectly neutral relation to desire,
like a star. She doesn't hold up the cup

and say, *Drink*. She doesn't tell me
to put it down either. If I say goodbye

to everybody, she loves me
or doesn't just the same.

APPARITION

At the kitchen sink, trimming the lower blooms
from forsythia I've cut in the front garden,
starting to set them into the low thick glass vase,

and my father says, *Mark is making the house pretty.*

He didn't speak to me the last five years of his life;
why should I be surprised he'd use the third person now?
Though he did make sure I heard him, didn't he—
he did say my name so that I could hear him,

and I think it was in gentleness, a compliment, and not in
mockery.

GOD-BOX

They give us a white cube, a paper box,
the kind that might hold a small gift,
and ask us to write or draw on its surface
our image of the divinity, whatever
that might be.
                        We're here, we have,
in principle, already agreed.
Daniel's octopus is a Buddha,
Glenn's highest self a blazing star,
though no marker's adequately golden.
In my future blue one hand blooms
from the next in a rush of wind
from another life.
                        Step two: Write
on an index card what you most want
to be released from, fold it,
place it inside, close the lid. That's it,
that's the end of the exercise.

Walking home on Sixth, thinking
it's intention not artifact that matters,
I'm inclined to toss the thing away,
but I wind up walking blocks
holding this coffer only a little bigger

than my hand. Steam blurs
a bank's bright windows;
glassy slab of winter twilight
over the stairs to the subway,
then I'm down in the station, restless,
walking the long platform,
                            and here's
the unknowable of music too far
to name. Keep walking, a violin,
sonorous, emotive. Closer: resolute travelers
facing the tracks but the rest of us
turn toward the man whose powers
concentrate on his instrument,
from which pours
                    —how is it possible?—
an aching distillate so exact
I don't need to go anywhere.
CD for sale in the velvet cavity
beside his shoes, two dollar bills,
gleaming change.
                    Odd bit of movement
across the tracks, so I can't help but look
toward the platform: a tall black man
—why does his darkness
seem to matter?—cradling a violin
that isn't there, invisible chin-rest
beneath his jaw, immaterial body resting
on the shoulder of his coat, and the bow
that isn't there lifted and lowered
precisely.
            Not mimicry; he knows the music.

On my side of the double tracks
the tunnel fills with an embodied grief,
too poised to be an outcry, contained,
larger than any single suffering,
and the man on the other side
makes nothing, no sound at all,
but answers adequately.

What did I write on that card?
One blue hand folding out of another,
one golden octopus,
one embattled star,
this box in these hands,
that have done so much
to harm myself,

this box.

UNDERWORLD

The new and towering boy in outpatient
folds the lavish scaffold of himself
into a smallish chair as though

it were an ongoing task
to account for all his parts
and he takes us in,

nods his smudge of beard
and smiles privately.
We've confirmed his expectations

—no malice or irony in it,
simply a kind of sweetness.
He's failed to kill himself

last weekend, and has landed
intact, marveling, interested,
his legs (I want to spell *long*

with two *n*'s, as Milton spelled
dim with a double *m*
to intensify the gloom of hell),

craning into one another
then pushing his knees forward
into the speaking circle

where we weigh
ninety minutes
the tonnage of our shame,

the damage yours
only until exactly spoken.
Whose pain's not a common one?

And then the new man
—all of twenty-two—stretches
his legs entirely forward

and catches my breath
with the name printed across
the tongues of his shoes:

OSIRIS, in bold letters,
maybe a brand too newly stylish
for me to have registered,

but the unlaced word prays
for us to just the right god:
Him torn to pieces,

each bit of His ruin picked up
each nearly unrecognizable
attended carried and mourned

and is it loved or willed
back into place: the man and boy's
body radiantly restored.

Or that's the hope he's poking
out at us, with his excellent shoes,
while we go on talking until lunchtime.

ARS POETICA:
14th Street Gym

Beauty that does not disguise the wound,
but reads through to the lack it marks:
the one-armed man lifts himself again

on the assisted pull-up machine,
sleeve of—sparrows?—and morning glories
swelling with each upward pull.

In the locker room, I praise his ink
and he turns—to thank me, and so I'll notice
(*what you can't restore, inscribe*)

the blue wing needled on the socket.

VERGE

A month at least before the bloom
and already five bare-limbed cherries

ringed in a haze of incipient fire:
right by the highway, middle of the afternoon,

a faint pink-bronze glow.
Some things wear their becoming:

the night we walked, nearly strangers,
from a fevered party to the corner

where you'd left your motorcycle,
afraid some rough wind might knock it

to the curb, you stood on the other side
of the upright bike, the other side of what

would be us, tilted your head toward me
over the wet leather seat while you strapped

your helmet on, engineer boots firm
on the black pavement. Did we guess

we'd taken the party's fire with us,
somewhere behind us that dim apartment

cooling around its core like a stone?
Can you know, when you're not even

a bud, but poised at some brink?
My April corona of new color,

visible echo troubling the air
by the roadway, little ripples of energy

so new they're almost imagined . . .
Could anyone driving in the departing gust

and spatter on Seventh
have seen some cloud breathed out

around us, as if we were a pair
of—could it be—soon-to-flower trees?

ROBERT HARMS PAINTS THE
SURFACE OF LITTLE FRESH POND

Surface the action of the day,

a means of tracing the dynamic,
so that a jitter of blue's
sparked by little coals,

sun a glimmer
of the day's intent. He knows
to trace an alphabet on water

is to surface the action of the day,

a way of proceeding,
entering into the never-
to-be-repeated,

a way of reading
a nearly infinite variety of gestures
legible only to one versed

in surface, the action of the day.

When my eye nearly failed
—the frail foil-back torn,
wild profusion of smoke-curls,

what I saw was just this:
what he sees on and in water,
by his hand

the action of surface notated,

the rhythm of things
discerned and ridden.

PESCADERO

The little goats like my mouth and fingers,

and one stands up against the wire fence, and taps on the
    fence-board
a hoof made blacker by the dirt of the field,

pushes her mouth forward to my mouth,
so that I can see the smallish squared seeds of her teeth,
    and the bristle-whiskers,

and then she kisses me, though I know it doesn't mean
    "kiss,"

then leans her head way back, arcing her spine, goat yoga,
all pleasure and greeting and then good-natured indiffer-
    ence: She loves me,

she likes me a lot, she takes interest in me, she doesn't
    know me at all
or need to, having thus acknowledged me. Though I am all
    happiness,

since I have been welcomed by the field's small envoy, and
  the splayed hoof,
fragrant with soil, has rested on the fence-board beside my
  hand.

NOT WITHOUT

That rectangle of meadow on Fireplace Road,
built entirely of a single grass that shades, near the top,
retriever-blonde or russet:
not without that, no.

Dim sheet of black bay water, on the south ferry,
hood of the car pulled right to the prow-rope,
the fogged lamps of where we're headed drawing nearer.
Not without those.

And Ned thundering toward me, when he's turned from
      whatever
and suddenly remembers I'm here, bounding into my aura
with a visible single-mindedness: that.

And Alex: the dear ache in his face which in turn makes
      me ache with fellow-feeling and desire.

The way that nothing in Vermeer has an edge; you could
      not describe this
adequately, nothing would ever allow you to see it.

Even when my eye first failed, in a Belgian restaurant on
      17th Street,

and the air filled with swirls of dark smoke, elegant
in their scrolling progression,

or the next day, when it began to snow in my right eye,

and even later, when I was blind and Sixth Avenue
was elongated and distorted, and pink
because I saw through a haze

of my own blood, and now and then a color
swam toward me like something carried on a flood tide.

Even that. Endless gratitude,
for the thing I would without be no one I know.

APPARITION

Bitter wind off the metal harbor
and here's Dugan crossing 15th Street
as if he owned it, sharp new jacket
just the shade of that riffled steel

—why shouldn't the dead
sport a little style?
                          Once, at a dinner
in his honor, I watched bored Dugan
take out a pair of clippers and begin to trim

his nails, till a fat yellow paring flew
and landed in the plate of his publisher's wife,
who screamed. Then the recalcitrant old boho
grew courtly, and with a smile that may

have been sincere, managed to convince her
he was a gentleman after all.
And here he is in the afterlife,
big glasses gleaming, standing up straight

as he never could in the years I knew him,
no chip on *his* shoulder
—you can tell by the shiny jacket
he's over all that now.

WHAT IS THE GRASS?

On the margin
in the used text
I've purchased without opening

—pale green dutiful vessel—

some unconvinced student has written,
in a clear, looping hand,
Isn't it grass?

How could I answer the child?
I do not exaggerate,
I think of her question for years.

And while first I imagine her the very type
of the incurious, revealing the difference
between a mind at rest and one that cannot,

later I come to imagine that she
had faith in language,
that was the difference: she believed

that the word settled things,
the matter need not be looked into again.

And he who'd written his book over and over, nearly
    ruining it,
so enchanted by what had first compelled him
—for him the word settled nothing at all.

INERADICABLE MUSIC

He had composed his great poems
in a kind of trance, he said,
to which he could no more will himself
to return . . . He's who sleeping,

could he shock himself awake?
And even if he writes now
some puffed-up simulation
—a sentimental elegy,

an ode to the state—
he knows they're still true,
those outpourings that came
when no one was listening,

and though it is terrible
never to be subject
to those dictations again,
how much more so to have gone

unvisited, to have remained unwritten
by those cadences, though they left him
exhausted and consumed.

IMMANENCE

My ex says he likes to ride on the top level
of the George Washington Bridge,
because then he's closer to his Lord.
I say, but isn't God immanent,
and he says, that's true too, and I say,
well, how can you be any closer then?
He enjoys the mystery of contradiction,
likes being lifted up, while I think the highest
level of the bridge is terrifying;
I act as though I am brave, because
I understand that it's beautiful up here,
shockingly so, April pouring its gold
over the gathered Hudson,
but still I think of Rilke saying beauty's
the beginning of a terror we can hardly bear.
My ex would say it's the other way round,
terror the beginning of some radical beauty,
and he's happy, while I drive the appalling,
crowded lane, and he looks out over the edges,
humming a little, entirely pleased.

ROBINSON JEFFERS

Why think sun and stones less alive than sea lions,
why privilege proteins or the slow burn of carbohydrates,
is that the only life there is?

Or, he might say, fire and granite suffer as much as
    everything else,
it would be a diminishment not to think so.

Still, he'd walk the shore, evenings, with his bulldog
—bowlegs working to keep pace,
darting to the foam-line, distracted by pleasure,
racing to catch up again, delay then hurry,

the creature performing a cheerful little drama—
and the poet, who could not be wholeheartedly pleased
with anything human, he liked that too.

ITHACA

My ex adores the age of mechanical reproduction;
nearly every day he copies something he likes,
simply to add more beauty to the world.

I say I'm tired I'll just wait in the car.

Liquor store, ale signs, grimy ice along
the strip of parking lot: Bare utility. Battered sedans,
driver buying one beer, a case. Two partial trees,

stripped limbs held over the sidewalk

as if they're starving. I have believed
if the scales fell from our eyes we'd see the world
as it is, that the core-light never flags,

only our ability to perceive it, but just now

even the destination of the wandering hero,
long after the war that would be remembered forever,
even the home he sought's a weary,

butt-end place, no comfort but a drink, no beauty
in sight so you have to go copy some. I'm tired,

the windows with their sad intoxicants are tired,

Ithaca so over the long winter it can't hold

its shaggy head up anymore. Ruinous old century,
spilling into this one: liquor and lopped trees, sharp odors
of ice and gasoline. What are these Ithacas for? Century of
    my birth,

go to sleep now. Can't we be done with you?

THE LESSON

Some workers put up a wall on 25th Street,
plywood sheathing a frame of two-by-fours to seal the
    building
they'd gut and remake. Then they added layers:

stacked metal pipe bound with black webbing
a skim of permits, photocopied signatures far removed
from whatever hand inscribed them.

Then a blue expanding ladder, hydraulic,
squatting on its haunches. John took pictures
of the whole unlikely and elaborate composition,

barrier and advertisement. How could you not
look at it, with its tears and concealments?
In this way I began to see walls: decaled plexi

between my face and the back of the cabdriver's head;
blue shroud on 16th like the robe of Venus rippling
over the entry of Pottery Barn, and inside it a grinder

scouring away at the stone. The insidious barrier—
who could put their hands on it?—dividing me
and the dark young men on my corner, smoking by the door

of the technical school. A story one of my teachers told,

her voice slipping to a register we'd never heard
in our room's calm rows: how a lover, desperate

to reach his beloved on the other side, strapped himself
beneath a car, face pressed up into the undercarriage,
the back of his head inches above the pavement.

How he'd tried to refuse, with his own body,
the sundering of his city. Did he live, did he ever arrive?
I remember only my teacher beginning to weep;

we didn't understand, what was the lesson?
John's pictures brought that back—and how,
decades later, the night they first scaled the wall,

the people at the top reached down to pull
the others up, and shouted, Come on, come on!
When the guards turned the water cannons on them,

they sprayed back from open bottles of champagne.
Then the broken chunks appeared, in the hands
of those who had loosened them, fragments

glazed with sprayed inscriptions,
scarred with sledgehammer and chisel:
instruments of union.

A demanding beauty about them,
whatever was scrawled perhaps capable
of realigning, as words in what language?

Something barely spoken yet.

TO JACKSON POLLOCK

Last night somebody murdered a young tree on Seventh
    Avenue
between 18th and 19th—only two in that block,
and just days ago we'd taken refreshment in the crisp and
    particular shade

of that young ginkgo's tight leaves, its beauty and optimism,
though I didn't think of that word until the snapped trunk
    this morning,
a broken broomstick discarded, and tell me what pleasure

could you take from that? Maybe I understand it,
the sudden surge of rage and the requirement of a gesture,
but this hour I place myself firmly on the side of thirst,

the sapling's ambition to draw from the secret streams
beneath this city, to lift up our subterranean waters.
Power in a pointless scrawl now on the pavement.

Pollock, when he swung his wild arcs in the barn-air
by Accabonac, stripped away incident and detail till all
that was left was swing and fall and return,

austere rhythm deep down things, beautiful
because he's subtracted the specific stub and pith,
this wreck on the too-hot pavement where scavengers

spread their secondhand books in the scalding sunlight.
Or maybe he didn't. Erase it I mean: look into the fierce
    ellipse
of his preserved gesture, and hasn't he swept up every bit,

all the busted and incomplete, half-finished and lost?
Alone in the grand rooms of last century's heroic painters
—granted entrance, on an off day, to a museum

with nobody, thank you, this once nobody talking—
for the first time I understood his huge canvases
were prayers. No matter to what. And silent as hell;

he rode the huge engine of his attention toward silence,
and silence emanated from them, and they would not take no
for an answer, though there is no other. Forget supplication,

beseechment, praise. Look down
into it, the smash-up swirl, oil and pigment and tree-
    shatter:
tumult in equilibrium.

DEEP LANE

Trying to pick radishes before the rain begins,
though the verb's not right; *pick*'s a quick and singular jab
of an action, when what's required

is to squat and peer among the ragged leaf-towns
for dome-tops risen dusty ruby or scarlet, eggshell or violet,

and then to grasp the whorl at the base and yank
upward, lightly, so the whole plant lifts
in a sweet-scented loose clump,

good mineral dirt falling from the white roots
and the accomplishment at their center: jewel-toned,

Russian somehow, artful, varied, contradicting Leonardo,
who wrote that nature does nothing unnecessary;
how would he account for this two-toned cylinder,

voguish red giving way, near the tip,
to a ghost-swath of muslin . . .

Then the first unsettling rumble
through the spatter
that's begun to muddy

then wash our hands, gathering body
until it suddenly seems to pass, like a wave, through the
    clutches

of radishes we're holding,
and then we can feel it, in our own hands:
the force that rings the air,

drives through silt possibility from nothing into wet
    dirt-speckled presence:
the two impossible bundles of thunder we're holding.

MEADOW CHURCH

After we walked the narrow gravel road across the hayfield,
mowed in late autumn, and not yet sprouted again,
and made our way up the slope smelling of soil
and long-cut grasses and cold, and of the stripped pine of
    the rail fence,

and approached the heavy doors, with their black metal
    banding
and heavy hinges, and peered in the amber window from
    the vestibule
and waited a time for the mass to end, we entered the white
    church

—a neutral, sturdy bulk from the field below—
nearly at closing, with just a few minutes to look
before someone would hurry us away. One breathless
    sweep,
and I thought I had never seen any built thing so lovely.

Around a glass box of pain—old icon, a crude Savior
    stumbling
toward us, weeping and bleeding—rose a world
entirely white, stippled in rose and sky, garlanded,

lighthearted, an upswirling baroque edifice of—say it—
comedy. Even the saints were chinoiserie! As if *this*
were what was required: to build around suffering
a liquid, airy music, effortless rondure

made to hold configuring forces to account.
A floating lightness allows us to draw near
a molten core, a measure of pain makes joy real?

My life with the man beside me solidified then,
found its footing. In the Wieskirche, in March,
not spring yet—while the church around us,
never for a moment still, became that moment

and onward what it aspired to,
a breathing cloud
of stone. We were together then.

THIS YOUR HOME NOW

For years I went to the Peruvian barbers on 18th Street
—comforting, welcome: the full coatrack,
three chairs held by three barbers,

eldest by the window, the middle one
a slight fellow who spoke an oddly feminine Spanish,
the youngest last, red-haired, self-consciously masculine,

and in each of the mirrors their children's photos,
mildly smutty cartoons, postcards from Machu Picchu.
I was happy in any chair, though I liked best

the touch of the oldest, who'd rest his hand
against my neck in a thoughtless, confident way.
Ten years maybe. One day the powdery blue

steel shutters pulled down over the window and door,
not to be raised again. They'd lost their lease;
I didn't know how at a loss I'd feel—

this haze around what I'd like to think
the sculptural presence of my skull
requires neither art nor science,

but two haircuts on Seventh, one in Dublin,
nothing right.
        Then (I hear my friend Marie
laughing over my shoulder, saying *In your poems*

there's always a then, and I think, *Is it a poem
without a then?*) dull early winter, back on 18th,
upspiraling red in a cylinder of glass, and just below the line

of sidewalk, a new sign, WILLIE'S BARBERSHOP.
Dark hallway, glass door, and there's (presumably)
Willie. When I tell him I used to go down the street

he says in an inscrutable accent, *This your home now*,
puts me in a chair, asks me what I want and soon he's
    clipping
and singing with the radio's Latin dance tune.

That's when I notice Willie's walls,
though he's been here all of a week, spangled with images
hung in barbershops since the beginning of time:

lounge singers, near-celebrities, random boxers
—Italian boys, Puerto Rican, caught in the hour
of their beauty, though they'd scowl at the word—

victors cheering over a trophy won for what?
Frames already dusty, at slight angles,
here, it's clear, forever. Are barbershops

like aspens, each sprung from a common root
ten thousand years old, sons of one father,
flashing fighters and starlets to shield the tenderness

at their hearts? Our guardian Willie defies time,
his chair our ferryboat, and we go down in the trance
of touch and the skull-buzz drone

singing cranial nerves in the direction of peace,
and so I understand that in the back
of this nothing building on 18th Street
                              —I've found that door ajar

before, in daylight, when it shouldn't be,
some forgotten bulb left burning in a fathomless shaft
of my uncharted nights—
                              the men I have outlived

await their turns, the fevered and wasted, whose mothers
and lovers scattered their ashes and gave away their clothes.
Twenty years and their names tumble into a numb well

—though in truth I have not forgotten one of you,
may I never forget one of you—these layers of men,
arrayed in their no-longer-breathing ranks.

Willie, I have not lived well in my grief for them;
I have lugged this weight from place to place
as though it were mine to account for,

and today I sit in your good chair, in the sixth decade
of my life, and if your back door is a threshold
of the kingdom of the lost, yours is a steady hand

on my shoulder. Go down into the still waters of this chair
and come up refreshed, ready to face the avenue.
Maybe I do believe we will not be left comfortless.

After everything comes tumbling down or you tear it
    down
and stumble in the shadow-valley trenches of the moon,
there's still a decent chance at—a barbershop,

salsa on the radio, the instruments of renewal wielded,
effortlessly, and, who'd have thought, for you.
Willie if he is Willie fusses much longer over my head

than my head merits, which allows me to be grateful
without qualification. Could I be a little satisfied?
There's a man who loves me. Our dogs. Fifteen,

twenty more good years, if I'm a bit careful.
There's what I haven't written. It's sunny out,
though cold. After I tip Willie

I'm going down to Jane Street, to a coffee shop I like,
and then I'm going to write this poem. Then

DEEP LANE

November and this road's tunnel
of soft fire draws you forward, as it descends,
as if you were moving toward

—radical completion,
some encompassment? Dark kindness
woven in the fabric of the afternoon.

And because you've held within your own veins
another passage of fire—obliterating mercy—
not these lit-up leaf-clouds

but a hot wire stealing into
the deepest chambers of the night—
you love the way the asphalt lifts

then hurries down toward Deep Lane.
The fire-road inside
is only that road once;

though desire sends you back there again
and again, it won't be that one you're on;
and thus you want all the harder.

So let this road take you,
autumn's enchanted boy
lifted into the wet-yellow lamps of the maples;

taken up by that fleeting light,
let your trophies fall to the rain,
let the lean of the motorbike

carry you down the moraine,
across the rising chill from the fields, on into town:
warm light, voices, a meal in the tavern's golden cave.

You won't be riding that other road much again,
but this one: the kind man's dark leather back
in front of you, the cycle's center of gravity

sinking lower, the delicious clay-cold of the field
between here and home rising up, scent of hay,
of animals and ruin. He knows

you would just as soon stay,
but lucky he's not here for that.
He ferries you home, maybe every night of your life.

Or that's what you wish he could do,
though you know it's you leaning against him
that makes your mutual direction.

Every night a little like the one he came home late,
happy, from the leather bar, and you in your welling up
out of sleep said, I have a lake in me,

and he looked at you closely, with a generous,
unflinching scrutiny, undeceived, loving, as clear a gaze
as anyone had ever brought to you, and he said, You do.

SPENT

Late August morning I go out to cut
spent and faded hydrangeas—washed
greens, russets, troubled little auras

of sky, as if these were the very silks
of Versailles, mottled by rain and ruin
then half-restored, after all this time . . .

When I come back with my handful
I realize I've accidentally locked the door,
and can't get back into the house.

The dining room window's easiest;
crawl through beauty bush and spirea,
push aside some errant maples, take down

the wood-framed screen, hoist myself up.
But how, exactly, to clamber across the sill
and the radiator down to the tile?

I try bending one leg in, but I don't fold
readily; I push myself up so that my waist
rests against the sill, and lean forward,

place my hands on the floor and begin to slide
down into the room, which makes me think
this was what it was like to be born:

awkward, too big for the passageway . . .
Negotiate, submit?
            When I give myself
to gravity there I am, inside, no harm,

the dazzling splotchy flowerheads
scattered around me on the floor.
Will leaving the world be the same

—uncertainty as to how to proceed,
some discomfort, and suddenly you're
—where? I am so involved with this idea

I forget to unlock the door,
so when I go to fetch the mail, I'm locked out
again. Am I at home in this house,

would I prefer to be out here,
where I could be almost anyone?
This time it's simpler: the window-frame,

the radiator, my descent. Born twice
in one day!
            In their silvered jug,
these bruise-blessed flowers:

how hard I had to work to bring them
into this room. When I say *spent*,
I don't mean they have no further coin.

If there are lives to come, I think
they might be a littler easier than this one.

AMAGANSETT CHERRY

Praise to the cherry on the lawn of the library,
the heave and contorted thrust of it, a master,
on its own root, negating the word *weeping*

(miles to the nearest tears),
requiring instead *down-fountaining*,
or *descending from a ferocious intention.*

Whatever twists the trunk
subsumed into pink explosiveness, and then, all summer,
the green-black canopy. Prefer it unbent?

I have no use for you then,
says the torque and fervor of the tree.